CRUNCH

Anamaría Crowe Serrano

To Loraa,
So lovely to meet you
in Vigo at Premaria 2018.
Un abrazo—
Anamaria
30/6/2018.

CRUNCH

First published 2018

Turas Press

6-9 Trinity Street

Dublin 2.

ISBN: 978-0-9957916-2-6

Cover design by Reads – Angie Crowe

Interior Typesetting by Printwell Design, Dublin 3

Printed in Ireland by

SPRINTprint

Also by Anamaría Crowe Serrano

BOOKS IN ENGLISH

CORRUPT PRESS
KALEIDOgraph
one columbus leap

SHEARSMAN BOOKS
on words and up words
Femispheres

EMPIRIA
Paso Doble

DELTA EDIZIONI
The Interpreter

TRANSLATIONS

(Chelsea Editions)
Instructions on How to Read a Newspaper, by V. Magrelli
Other Signs, Other Circles, by A. Ferramosca
Mindskin, by A. Zagaroli
Paradigm: New and Selected Poems, by A. de Palchi

(Gradiva Publications)
Poetic Dialogue with T.S. Eliot's Four Quartets, by L. Celi
Selected Poems, by D. Raimondi
Selected Poems, by A. Toni

(amazon.com)
Killing Pythagoras, by M. Chicot

(Shearsman)
Beyond the Sea, by Elsa Cross

The self is made manifest in the opposites and the conflicts between them; it is a coincidentia oppositorum. Hence the way to the self begins with conflict.

(*Psychology* 186) – Carl Jung

Disloyalty has its place too

Eamonn Lynskey

skinpeel

blitzblend

wholeheal

asitwas

fervent

shallbe

sugarstarch

sunsweet

wholehigh

asitwere

ferment

nowthen

behold
theleafasitgrows
silentleafgreenly
innocentleafguilty
s   falls
t   leaffalls
e   an
apple m **apple**
thisjuicyoctoberistempting
clingingtoficklesteminthebelieftha
ttherewillbegrowththattherewillbepr
ogressbutwhatisprogressifnottheneed
tofeelalivewhensucculentoctobercomes
tothinkthereissomethingworthbeinghere
forthatthereismoremorebehindthesurface
somethingsymbolicathirdorevenfourthdim
ensionsomethingworthbitingworthsometh
ingworthfillingtheemptyspacethatisleftw
henthe**apple**fallswhenthebranchisbared
andthewormisrevealedbutthe**apple**will
neverbeenoughitsnectardrippinginth
egreentheinnocentfarawayfieldthe
onewecanneverreachtheonewor
thhavingworthdrippingforwort
hriskingeverythingforworth
blindleaffightingforbrav
eleafclingingclinging
forwhatit'sworth

I was neither Eve
nor Adam
in the garden of Eden
nor the arguments between them
over who
and why

I was the apple
bitten
tossed aside
her teeth marks
still on my flesh
her fingerprints
warm
on my skin

Go on,
bite me
it's already been done
I'm crunchy, sweet
ripe
and ready for retribution

the apple
looks innocent
dangling
on a tree
that has never
been pruned

innocent
    of Newton
    of the doctor
    of William Tell
    of someone's eye

but the apple
succumbs
to gravity
the worm of doubt
and disease
to arrows of all kinds
especially those of love

                    innocently
it succumbs
to the memory
of the garden
etched in the core
we cut out
and throw away

I know what it's like
to be the apple
of her eye   night
and day her foremost
thought
          the drive
to turn complacency
on its head

I know what it's like
to see the plot unfolding
in the shape of her hand
reaching out to me
such intensity of purpose
overriding fear

          her impulse to bite
          is a test
          not of virtue
          but intelligence

when she looks at me
she can tell there is
more worth knowing
than the pampering
that goes on in paradise

she can tell
I am the key
to the secrets
of the universe

it is why I am so edible
to her discerning eye
as she examines me now
in the palm of her hand

she lifts me to her face
but it will still take
a leap of faith
for her to bite

here

like this   *fingers* barely touching the ridges of my skin   these tactile rugae that hold oils and hints of light   glints of ivory falsehoods   how can this be you or me?

     fingers tilting me to obscurity   yes, a little further from view   to the darkness of a gaze that believes none of it   the darkness of an ignorance that believes it all

     fingers light   there must be no sensuality in this   you couldn't get your nipples to look less naughty, could you?   fingers lingering   almost as if untouching me

     fingers on a hand detached from body   though looming from your womb echoing your ripeness   in such a way that the eye falls on many myths   mistruths   salacious hues

     fingers slightly parted   though not immediately obvious as two *fingers* while simultaneously suggesting come hither   can you do that   it's essential to the story

never mind

     fingers on the other hand now   limp   a slaughtered lamb   draining from the body   framing your distended belly   without intent   this new modesty reeking of boredom

     fingers far from me   crawling into the nethers of the garden   you and me equal and opposite temptations in this endless telling   that's good

     fingers self-sufficient despite being relegated to the edge of the world   performing all the body's needs   an innocence too threatening

she is named, her children
named, and her children's
children, a long lineage

branching, forking, fruits
of multiplication recorded
in papyrus for posterity

she is the root of my neglect
while I remain unnamed
merely used so as to be

abused – but I am more
than the butt of a universal
joke, I am the very core

of philosophies invented
for her to believe in, fall
over and over into amnesia

by the skin of her teeth
she clings to the memory
of herself as truth, daughter

of the earth, mistress
          of paradise

I've borne her
long enough
under my skin

her darkness
shifts

somewhere
innocence
must self-destruct

the road to paradise
is slippery
lined with prohibition
treacherous piths

where fall
gets conjugated
in the sinful
in the plural
in the pluperfect subvertive
in the entirely conditional
in the disjunctive
and even then
or maybe because of then
it never truly conforms
to verb, action
exponential to the cause
– apple –
which is both agent and object
and none of these,
being anachronistic
not even figuratively related
to fig or quince
certainly not to Eve
though syncopal fruit that it is
conveniently parses
with ale

32

fall (noun) :

      a return to earth   loam and stomachs of birds   ;

my seed   destined for the ground   how else would i fruit
                  height (essential)

;   a beginning   more winding the path   less simple   unsafe
           rock   bottom

    ;   vulnerability   knowledge
that things may crack crumble decay shrivel divide decline   permanently   ;
                  impermanence
                also implies aspiration

persistent   belief in more   ;   open to serpents

     ; navigation of her divine little hand to her profane little mouth
     her story the starting point of his

before any of that
this was just a garden

flora   fauna
before the words for names

and I   the shyest
no more or less
but noteworthily nameless and not
what you think   not
shapely or entirely edible

bitter back then
thin-skinned   hard-edged
stung by exclusion
segregated
for my difference

as far as I'm concerned
it was just an excuse
to wield some power
in Eden before Eve
got wise
and reclaimed the lot

En el sueño del hombre que soñaba, el soñado se despertó.

(Las ruinas circulares—Jorge Luis Borges)

long before they were here i understood that the violence of creation contained a
fundamental paradox   a flaw that could only lead to a fall   it was clear from the
garden   its dreamy treasures   finite yet spreading to infinity   and i wished i had known
the all-seeing at the height of the frenzy   day and night the thought sucked me dry and
everything that had seemed bounteous took on the oblique discomfort of a curse

the man   alone or cradled by the woman was null   insubstantial as the leaves he later
pulled to hide his shame

the man   defiling the virgin earth

one of them would have to set all the laws in motion   recalibrate the dichotomies
one of them would have to move beyond the confines and probe wider sense

she rose one afternoon without him   entered the telling through the labyrinth of leaves
and sick of its goading flung the snake aside   as she reached for me i saw the aleph
burning in her eyes

I will go mad

malic grief undoing

the simplest joys   eternity undoing itself

on her tongue

the woman who   eyes and fruit   for her husband
both of them   of the fig   he ate leaves
took was naked   ate together and   that gave coverings

and also of   opened the She   then they were
the tree for   and they made   sewed to themselves
her eye saw   so desirable good   and when she

to the wisdom   it was food   took some they
and realized   for some gaining   were also pleasing
                                       with it

it cannot be described –
                the sky inverting

the fruit
in her smile
saying it all

she stumbles   into a run

shouting

        the terror of things –

duplicitous plants

          spying

    shameless animals   ogling

    who knows when the garden will end
        the confines are all too clear

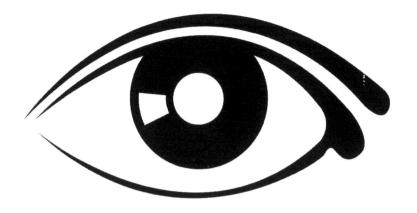

who saw her   sick or mad

      the flower suffering its own
             insanity

akn

otofsn   who can say my fellow

akes   blossoms did not collude

                                sicker still this tree

you too

                        but maybe not ---------

you're probably busy putting your house in order

The last thing   her footsole dustcaked   solestamped mud

imprint of perfection parted

imperfect

where

?

what imparted   ?

to reach her   if only   branchleaf   barksap   call her back

to know   at least

what was folly   to know

if

was it foolish to grow proud when I would fade

my airs bruised   inside|out

and hers –

pitted against may and hem

and woe and men

– struggling to dance

what now   ...   my raison d'être shrivels

                    perhaps to be a slice of art

                                        a muse

victim of a hunger   nuance that passes for truth

what is the garden now

            its juices exposed   ...   delighting

        in chaos   ...

        a first fractal no doubt

                    all animal all earth

https://www.youtube.com/watch?v=pbWCifikhVM

the UNBELIEVERS

lie   say   i   did not exist

                 i   say   time

          will tell

Acknowledgements

The fact that this collection exists is entirely due to the encouragement of Liz McSkeane, Eamonn Lynskey and Ross Hattaway, who saw its potential when I had given up on it. In particular, I am indebted to Liz for including me as a Turas Press author, for her enthusiasm and help with the layout and logistics.

I am very grateful to the editors of journals that have supported my work over the years and where some of these poems appear. They include *Flare, Poetry Ireland Review, Shearsman, Tears in the Fence, The Pickled Body, The Stony Thursday Book*.

While I was half way through writing these poems I had the good fortune to join the amazing Friends of James Joyce Tower Society who did a weekly reading of *Finnegans Wake* at Fitzgerald's pub in Sandycove, guided by Robert Walsh's extraordinary erudition. Some of the energy of that group, along with the odd word and idea from the *Wake* – not least the number 32 – has crept into the later poems.

Biographical Note

Anamaría Crowe Serrano is an Irish poet and translator of Spanish and Italian to English. As well as having been anthologised and published widely in journals in Ireland and abroad, publications include *KALEIDOgraph* (corrupt press, 2017), written with Greek poet Nina Karacosta, *on words and up words* (Shearsman, 2016), one columbus leap (corrupt press, 2011), *Femispheres* (Shearsman, 2008), and *Paso Doble* (Empirìa, 2006), written with Italian poet Annamaria Ferramosca. She also wrote poems for the art catalogue Mirabile Dictu (blurb, 2011).

In recent years, she has been involved in several collaborations with other poets, including the Upstart project in Dublin, Steven Fowler's "Yes, But Are We Enemies?" project, and Robert Sheppard's EUOIA (European Union of Imaginary Authors) project which was published by Shearsman in October 2017 under the title *Twitters for a Lark*.

Anamaría's translations have been published internationally.
For more information, browse http://anamariacs1.wix.com/amcs.